SHAKESPEARE RETOLD

RICHARD III

by

Martin Waddell & Alan Marks

W
FRANKLIN WATTS

First published in 2008
by Franklin Watts
338 Euston Road
London NW1 3BH

Franklin Watts Australia
45–51 Huntley Street
Alexandria
NSW 2015

Text copyright © Martin Waddell 2008
Illustrations copyright © Alan Marks 2008
Notes copyright © Franklin Watts 2008

Editor: Jackie Hamley
Series design: Peter Scoulding

A CIP catalogue record for this book is available from
the British Library.

ISBN: 978 0 7496 7745 9 (hbk)
ISBN: 978 0 7496 7752 7 (pbk)

Printed in China

Fnanklin Watts is a division of
Hachette Children's Books,
an Hachette Livre UK company.
www.hachettelivre.co.uk

CONTENTS

THE CAST

The House of York

King Edward IV

Duchess of York – his mother

Edward and Richard – his sons, the princes

George, Duke of Clarence – his brother

Richard, Duke of Gloucester – his brother

Queen Elizabeth – King Edward's wife

Earl Rivers – her brother

Dorset and Gray – her sons from an earlier marriage

The House of Lancaster

Queen Margaret – widow of King Henry VI

Henry Tudor – Earl of Richmond

***

Duke of Buckingham – Richard's supporter

Sir William Catesby – Richard's supporter

Lord Hastings – Lord Chamberlain

Lord Stanley – Earl of Derby, Hastings' friend

PROLOGUE

A ruthless man plots to win the English
throne. There are murders, betrayals,
intrigues and executions as a bloodstained
rose twists round the Crown.

All ends on a field of battle,
where what was won is lost again.

This is the story of RICHARD III
who once was England's king.

CHAPTER ONE

ENTER A VILLAIN

The Wars of the Roses seemed to have ended in victory for the white rose of the house of York over the red rose of the house of Lancaster.

King Edward IV of York had defeated Henry VI of Lancaster in battle and taken the throne, helped by his brothers, George, Duke of Clarence, and Richard, Duke of Gloucester.

But Richard was envious of his older brothers, especially Edward the new king. "Now is the winter of our discontent made glorious summer by this son of York!" he sneered. He burned with ambition to seize the throne for himself. Then those who had mocked his ugly body would have cause to fear. "Born so ugly that dogs bark at me. I'll play the villain that they call me!" he told himself.

King Edward's two young sons and Clarence stood before him in the line of succession, and therefore between him and the throne. They must die or be got rid of if he were to be crowned king. It was as simple as that to a ruthless mind, and Richard's mind was ruthless.

First he moved against his brother Clarence. He secretly started a rumour that Clarence was plotting to overthrow the king. Clarence was arrested and taken to the Tower of London. Richard spoke to him before he went.

"Brother, we are not safe! The queen is using her influence over the king against us," he lied. "She hopes to win more power for her own family – her brother Earl Rivers and the sons of her first marriage, Dorset and Gray."

"Then no one is safe but the queen's own family," the fearful Clarence agreed. "What should we do?"

"We must pretend we are loyal to her," Richard told Clarence. "I will do it, to protect you."

"Poor simple Clarence," Richard smirked as his brother was led away to the Tower. "I love you so, that I will shortly send your soul to heaven!"

CHAPTER TWO

A WIDOW'S PROPHECY

Richard had to strengthen his position at court, if he were to win the throne.

The cunning Duke of Buckingham would be his ally, or so Richard thought. And the Lord Chamberlain, Hastings, had reason to distrust the queen. *If* Hastings took his side, Richard hoped that Hastings' friend Lord Stanley and other nobles would follow.

A summons from the king gave Richard an opportunity. King Edward was anxious to make sure that his eldest son, the Prince of Wales, would succeed him as king. Knowing of the hatred between the two powerful groupings at his court, he commanded Richard and the queen's family to appear in his presence and make peace.

But Richard wanted nothing of peace and went directly to the queen, when he heard this.

"Who told the king I hate them?" Richard confronted her in front of Hastings and the other nobles. "I do not flatter and smile and deceive, as others do… and this is my reward. My brother Clarence is imprisoned by your means, and I am disgraced!"

"The king acted by himself," the queen replied angrily. "Not on my advice."

Richard continued to protest. He argued that the queen's family had all been shown royal favour, though their loyalty to the king was questionable. Others, like himself, who had proved their loyalty in battle were ignored or sent to the Tower, as Clarence had been.

"We are loyal to King Edward," Rivers defended his sister, the queen, "just as we would be loyal to you, if you were our lawful king."

Hastings stood listening. Recently released from the Tower himself, he believed the queen and her family responsible for his imprisonment.

Surely he would back Richard? The careful Hastings gave nothing away.

Queen Margaret, widow of the dead
King Henry VI, joined in the quarrel,
cursing Richard and holding him
responsible for the death of her
husband and her son.

"Have done you withered hag!"
Richard hissed.

The watchful Buckingham
tried to stop her.

"Oh princely
Buckingham, my
friend, beware of
that dog Richard!"
the widow
warned. "Sin,
death and hell
have set
their marks
on him!"

"What does she say,
Buckingham?" Richard asked.

"Nothing I respect, my lord," Buckingham
answered, signalling clearly to everybody
that he was taking Richard's side.

"You scorn my advice," the furious widow
swore. "But remember my prophecy. All of you
will be subjects of his hate, and he of yours!"
She stormed out, cursing them all.

"Her curses make my hair stand on end!" Buckingham muttered.

"God pardon me. The widow Margaret has suffered a lot, and I spoke too harshly to her," Richard said, pretending to forgive her.

If Hastings and the others were taken in, Rivers was not. The queen's brother knew that forgiving his enemies was not in Richard's nature.

"I'm dealing with simple fools!" Richard congratulated himself when he was alone. "I sigh, and tell them that God bids us do good for evil… and they believe it! I hide my villainy and seem a saint, when I must play the devil."

CHAPTER THREE

TWO BROTHERS DIE

King Edward IV believed he was dying,
and he made it known that Richard would be
named Lord Protector. He would be in charge
of the country until the young Edward, Prince
of Wales, was old enough to rule.

The queen's family felt threatened by the
news, but no one was surprised.

It seemed that the wars between
the houses of York and
Lancaster might not be
finished after all. The
Lancastrian, Henry Tudor,
Earl of Richmond, was
rumoured to be
gathering an army
in France.

Richard was powerful enough to oppose Henry
if he tried to seize the throne for Lancaster.
The gentle Clarence was not, though Clarence
still stood next in line to the throne after the
young princes.

"If I am to be crowned, my brother Clarence
must die before the king!" Richard decided,
  and having decided he acted.

Secretly he had Clarence
    murdered in the Tower,
      drowned in a barrel of wine.

So it was that when Richard
and his rivals gathered in the
king's presence to make
peace, one powerful
player was missing.

"Clarence should be
here," the queen told
the king.

Richard pretended
to be angry.
"Why am I so
badly treated
in the king's
presence?"
he flared.
"You know
my poor
brother is
dead."

"Clarence, dead? But I sent an order for his release from the Tower!" King Edward groaned.

"Your order came too late," Richard lied easily.

The rivals made their peace... seemingly... and the sickly king stumbled to his deathbed.

CHAPTER FOUR

LORD PROTECTOR

"Send for the Prince of Wales!" Rivers advised the queen, after the death of the king. "Have your son crowned at once. You will not be safe until he is king."

"Let the prince be brought quietly to London," a scheming Buckingham advised. "The country is in a state of great unrest. It would be unwise to have him lead a great army of followers at this time. Without a king on the throne who knows what might happen."

Later, Buckingham spoke with Richard alone. "Whoever goes to fetch the prince, we two should not stay at home!" he advised. "The queen's proud family must be parted from him."

"I am as a child. I will do as you advise, dear cousin," Richard agreed, flattering Buckingham.

They intercepted the party the queen had sent to fetch the prince.

Buckingham and Richard had the queen's brother Rivers and her son Gray arrested and executed. The queen's other son Dorset escaped to France to join Henry Tudor, who was preparing to set sail for England with his army.

The two young princes were taken unwillingly to the Tower, to the horror of their frightened mother, the queen.

"It's for your own safety," their uncle Richard told them, though many doubted it.

CHAPTER FIVE

CUT OFF HIS HEAD!

Richard and Buckingham had power almost within their grasp, but they still had to reckon with the Lord Chamberlain Hastings and Lord Stanley.

They believed that Stanley would follow Hastings' lead… but would Hastings back Richard?

"What will we do if Hastings stands against us?" Buckingham asked.

"Cut off his head!" Richard said coldly, adding a bribe. "When I am king, I'll make you Earl of Hereford!"

"I'll hold you to that promise," Buckingham said.

Buckingham sent a man named Catesby to test Hastings. "The country is in chaos, my lord. If only Richard were on the throne…" Catesby began.

"I'd have my head cut from my shoulders before I'd agree to that!" Hastings swore.

"He has acted against your enemies, the queen's family, my lord," Catesby said pointing out that Rivers and Gray had already been executed.

"I can't mourn my enemies," Hastings said.
"But I won't take Richard's side against the lawful
heir either. God knows I will not do it."
His fate was sealed.

Next morning, at a meeting held to arrange the
coronation of the Prince of Wales, Richard
denounced the Lord Chamberlain,
accusing Hastings of conspiring
against him with the queen.

Hastings was
taken away to be
beheaded.

CHAPTER SIX

A KING IS CROWNED

Only Edward's sons, the young Prince of Wales and his little brother, now stood between Richard and the throne.

Richard, as Lord Protector, could not be seen to act against them, so the next move was Buckingham's.

The cunning statesman spread doubts about the two boys' right to the throne, suggesting that their father, King Edward, had not been properly married to the queen and, even if he had, there were doubts about his birth as well.

Buckingham argued that the citizens should demand that the true heir be king, however reluctant Richard might be to claim his rightful inheritance.

The mayor and citizens of London were convinced and came to beg Richard to take the throne.

They found him at prayer, in a scene well scripted with Buckingham beforehand.

"I am unfit for crown and majesty. It is against my conscience and my soul. God knows I don't desire it," Richard proclaimed, before allowing himself to be persuaded... exactly as he and Buckingham had planned.

Richard was proclaimed king with pomp and ceremony.

He had achieved his ambition.

But while the two young princes still lived, they remained a threat to their uncle.

"They must die quickly," Richard told Buckingham. "Do you agree?"

"I need time to think," Buckingham said, carefully.

"Now he stops for breath," Richard thought angrily, and he had the two young princes murdered in the Tower.

31

When Buckingham
came to claim his
promised earldom,
he paid the price
for his caution.

"I'm not in the mood
today!" Richard said,
dismissing him.

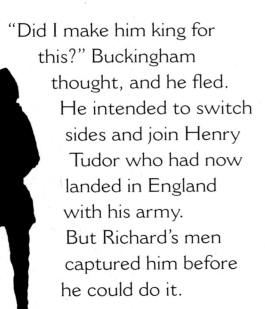

"Did I make him king for
this?" Buckingham
thought, and he fled.
He intended to switch
sides and join Henry
Tudor who had now
landed in England
with his army.
But Richard's men
captured him before
he could do it.

"Margaret's curse falls heavily upon my neck!" Buckingham groaned as he was led away to be executed on Richard's orders. "I should never have trusted him."

The widow Margaret's prophecy had come true.

CHAPTER SEVEN

BOSWORTH FIELD

The final battle between the white rose of York and the red rose of Lancaster was fast approaching, and fate seemed to have turned against Richard.

The queen's followers and many others flocked to join the Lancastrian army. Of the powerful nobles only a reluctant Lord Stanley remained, fearing for the life of his son who was held hostage by Richard.

Even Richard's mother, the Duchess of York, opposed him, angered by the death of Clarence and the murder of the two young princes, her grandchildren.

"You toad! You damned son! You came on earth to make my life a hell!" she told him. "I should have ended your life at birth. Bloody you are, and bloody will be your end!"

On the night before the battle the
two opposing armies rested close to
Bosworth Field, near Leicester.

Henry Tudor slept peacefully,
confident of winning.

Richard could not sleep. The ghosts
of those he had had murdered or
executed came to him, one after
the other – Clarence, Rivers, Gray,
Hastings and his two innocent
nephews in the Tower.

"Bloody and guilty! In bloody battle
end your days! Despair and die!"
they taunted.

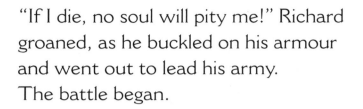

"If I die, no soul will pity me!" Richard groaned, as he buckled on his armour and went out to lead his army.
The battle began.

Richard fought bravely in his own cause, but the betrayer was himself betrayed when Lord Stanley delayed the advance of his men. He did not charge down the hill as planned, and Richard was left outnumbered.

His horse died underneath him, and Richard fell to the ground.

"A horse, a horse, my kingdom for a horse!" he cried despairingly as his enemies surrounded him.

The crown Richard had fought so hard to win lay in the mud of Bosworth field as Richard died.

The red rose of Lancaster had triumphed over
the white rose of York and the Wars of the Roses
had finally ended.

Henry VII was proclaimed king.

EPILOGUE

All ended on a field of battle,
where what was lost
was won again.

That was the story of
RICHARD III
who once was England's king.

NOTES

by Dr Catherine Alexander

Shakespeare wrote *Richard III* as the fourth in a series of history plays. The series began with the reign of King Henry VI and ended with the defeat of King Richard by Henry Richmond at the Battle of Bosworth. This was the last great battle of the Wars of the Roses, the English civil wars that lasted for thirty years.

The long period of history that the four plays cover is very complicated. *Richard III* can be difficult to follow because it refers to events that happened in the previous three plays. It also has a very large cast and is the second longest Shakespeare play. Yet from the moment

Shakespeare wrote it in the early 1590s it has always been one of his most popular plays.

The play was frequently reprinted from its first publication in 1597 onwards. Perhaps its popularity with the first audiences and readers was based partly on its patriotism: the victorious Henry Richmond (Henry VII) was the first Tudor king and Queen Elizabeth's grandfather. His final speech talks of uniting "the white rose and the red" and looks forward with hope to a long lasting peace.

The main reason for the play's lasting popularity, however, is its fascinating central character, Richard. In the very first speech of the play he announces to the audience, "I am determined to prove a villain," and watching how he sets about cheating, lying and killing to become king is very exciting. There is ambition, power and politics, an exploration of good and evil, superstition and a ghost scene. There is a great deal of death but only Richard dies on stage in his fight with Richmond at the end of the play. The other deaths are just reported.

Like the action, the language is also thrilling, and Richard is called a toad, a spider, a hedgehog, a dog, a hell-hound and a rooting hog. There is no sympathy in the play for what Richard calls his "own deformity". Indeed, he uses his physical ugliness as the excuse for his bad behaviour.